Resources for
an Uncertain Future

Resources for an Uncertain Future

**Papers presented at a Forum
marking the 25th anniversary
of Resources for the Future,
October 13, 1977, Washington, D.C.**

Charles J. Hitch, editor
Lewis M. Branscomb
Harrison Brown
Robert W. Fri
Paul W. MacAvoy
William H. McNeill
Edward S. Mason
Charles L. Schultze

Published for Resources for the Future
by The Johns Hopkins University Press
Baltimore and London

Library of Congress Catalog Card Number 77-18378
ISBN 0-8018-2105-3
ISBN 0-8018-2098-7 *paper*

Resources for the Future is a nonprofit organization for research and education in the development, conservation, and
use of natural resources and the improvement of the quality
of the environment. It was established in 1952 with the
cooperation of the Ford Foundation. Grants for research are
accepted from government and private sources only if they
meet the conditions of a policy established by the Board of
Directors of Resources for the Future. The policy states that
RFF shall be solely responsible for the conduct of the research and free to make the research results available to the
public. Part of the work of Resources for the Future is car-
ried out by its resident staff; part is supported by grants to
universities and other nonprofit organizations. Unless
otherwise stated, interpretations and conclusions in RFF
publications are those of the authors; the organization takes
responsibility for the selection of significant subjects for
study, the competence of the researchers, and their freedom
of inquiry.

This book was designed by Missy Lipsett.

RFF editors: Joan R. Tron, Ruth B. Haas, Jo Hinkel, and
Sally A. Skillings

Contents

Foreword

The papers published in this brief volume were prepared for presentation October 13, 1977, at a forum marking the 25th anniversary of the founding of Resources for the Future (RFF) as a non-profit research and educational organization. Since 1952 there has been a growing public awareness of resource and environmental problems and an enormous increase in the importance of these problems on the agenda of public policy. RFF has contributed substantially both to the public understanding of these issues and to the clarification of policy issues through the publication of some two hundred studies, as well as by speeches, seminars, and testimony by staff members. The purpose of the forum was to appraise, from a number of perspectives, the resource and environmental outlook for the United States during the next twenty-five years in the light of events of the recent past. What are offered here are informed opinions on selected issues rather than the kind of research that is customarily associated with RFF publications. We hope that the questions raised here will help stimulate discussion as we search for better ways to cope with an uncertain future.

Foreword

The views expressed here, as in all RFF publications, are those of the authors and are not to be interpreted as those of RFF staff members, officers, or directors.

Charles J. Hitch
President, Resources for the Future

Washington, D.C.

Resources for
an Uncertain Future

Resources in the Past and for the Future

Edward S. Mason

Dean Emeritus, Harvard University, and Honorary Member of the Board of Directors of Resources for the Future

My introduction to natural resource problems came during World War II, when I was employed as an economist in the Office of Strategic Services. For an economist in a wartime intelligence agency, one of the chief tasks was estimating the industrial and military production of the Central Powers, principally Germany. It became a continued and increasing source of astonishment to see how Germany, with relatively small supplies of metals and minerals, could achieve such large outputs of trucks, planes, munitions, and other war matériel—outputs that expanded steadily from 1939 to 1944, despite growing losses from aerial bombardment. The answer to this was fully revealed only after the war, largely as a result of the investigations of the U.S. Strategic Bombing Survey. It then became known that, although the consumption of copper in the United States during the war years was ten times that in Germany; of tin, twenty times; of manganese, ten times; of nickel, forty to fifty times; and of other scarce metals in proportion, Germany ended the war with larger stocks of most of these metals than she had in 1939.

How was this accomplished? It was done mainly by the substitution of relatively plentiful metals for relatively scarce ones; the redesigning of equipment in order to eliminate or to curtail scarce metal requirements; the extensive collection of scrap; and the paring down of civilian requirements.[1] Of particular interest were the technological possibilities of substitution that were involved in the redesigning of equipment. At the beginning of 1942 railway locomotives contained, on the average, 2.3 metric tons of copper, but by the middle of 1943 this had been reduced to 237 kilograms, or about one-tenth of the original amount. Early in the war the building of a submarine required 56 tons of copper; later this was reduced to 26 tons. The use of alloy steel was virtually eliminated from railway car construction, and iron radiators were substituted for copper radiators in all motor vehicles. In the use of ferro alloys, relatively plentiful vanadium and silicon were substituted for the less plentiful alloys. Vanadium was substituted for molybdenum in gun tubes under 21 centimeters in length. Nickel was replaced by vanadium in gun tubes under 10.5 centimeters in length. In addition, new processes were devised for working lower-grade ore supplies, such as chrome sources in the Balkans. And, of course, the very large quantities of scrap that exist in all highly industrial societies were assiduously collected and utilized.

It cannot be said that the German management of raw materials shortages was accomplished without cost. Obviously, labor inputs per unit of output were increased, and in some cases, no doubt, a certain loss in the quality of finished products was unavoidable. But it must be emphasized that, despite the scarcity of essential materials, the German war effort was not limited by a shortage of raw materials and that this very considerable transformation and substitution was accomplished in a relatively short period.

During a war emergency, of course, cost considerations are of relatively small importance. In Germany, technology was set free to do what could be done without worrying too much about price incentives and disincentives. Nevertheless, one could not help but be impressed that scarcity is a relative term, to be interpreted only with all the possibilities of substitution in mind.

After the war I wrote a number of articles on materials and national security,[2] and I suppose that these led to my next venture in the natural resources area, my membership on the President's Materials Policy Committee, the so-called Paley Commission, which published its final report, *Resources for Freedom*, in 1952. In those days you remember that everyone was for freedom—"Full Employment in a Free Society";

3

economic growth in a free society; and in a Harvard football program, the leading article was entitled "Football in a Free Society."

The Paley Report

The Paley Commission was appointed during one of those recurring periods in American history when a potential shortage of industrial materials seemed imminent. Consumption of materials during wartime had been stupendous, and whether or not the United States could look forward to rapid economic growth unimpeded by material shortages and what, if anything, we needed to do for security reasons, seemed to be questions worth investigating. Interest in these questions was currently heightened by the very large increase in materials prices occasioned by the Korean War. President Truman's letter of January 22, 1951, admonished the commission, "We cannot allow shortages of materials to jeopardize our national security nor to become a bottleneck to our economic expansion. The task of the Committee, therefore, will be to make an objective enquiry into all major aspects of the problem of assuring an adequate supply of production materials for our long-range needs and to make recommendations which will assist me in formulating a comprehensive policy on such materials."[3]

The commission did indeed make a large number of recommendations but, in the main, these were ignored as the postwar fear of materials shortages gave way to a comfortable complacency. The principal impact of the commission's report lay in its findings and methods of analysis, and the report is, perhaps, as interesting for what it ignored as for what it emphasized. Its primary tool of analysis, in dealing with prospective adequacy of supplies, lay in the concept of real costs. What would constrain economic growth was not, in the commission's view, the physical limits of discoverable supplies but the real costs of making those supplies available; that is, the real costs, measured either in the labor or capital inputs per unit of output or in the prospective price of materials in relation to changes in the general price level. If real costs were the constraint, an examination of the material limits to growth required more than a forecast of rates of consumption and a knowledge of existing and potential reserves. It required a study of the possibilities of substitution within a flexible price system and an estimation of the possibilities of technological innovation. A substantial part of the commission's report, therefore, was devoted to technology and to the possible effects of technological change on the redesigning of products and processes, the recycling of materials, the excavating of leaner ore bodies, and other applications bearing on what might happen to the real costs of materials.

The commission undertook a careful study of what had, in fact, happened to the real costs of mineral and agricultural raw materials during the period 1900–50 and came to the conclusion—surprising to most people—that for all groups, except forest products, the trend of real material costs was downward; and for many groups, strongly downward. So far from being a constraint on economic growth the declining costs of material inputs had been a growth accelerator. This effect was further enhanced, as the commission discovered, by the fact that the value of all material inputs constituted a persistently declining share of the GNP. As Barnett and Morse later calculated, the percentage of value added to the GNP, accounted for by the consumption of extractive production, mineral, and agriculture, declined from 45 percent in 1870 to 14 percent in 1957. As they point out, this decline over nearly a century marked, more or less, the transition from a preindustrialized society, oriented to raw materials production and consumption, to a highly industrialized society, oriented toward the fabrication of materials.[5]

It might have been thought that, since the commission found raw materials production and consumption constituted a declining share of total output and since the real cost per unit of materials output had been persistently falling, they would have concluded that all was well. Indeed, there was a tendency to come to this conclusion, but it was severely undermined by considerations of future uncertainties and the desire, at all costs, to be responsible statesmen. So the commission concluded, "Real costs of materials production have for some years been declining, and this decline has helped our living standards to rise. In this Commission's view, today's threat in the materials problem is that this downward trend in real costs may be stopped or reversed tomorrow—if indeed this has not already occurred."

In fact, as later studies have shown, this decline in the real costs of materials production and extraction per unit has continued, with minor exceptions, up to the present. Barnett and Morse carry the calculations to 1957, and Nordhaus computes the relationship of the prices of ten important minerals to the price of labor from 1900 to 1970. Their computations indicate "that there has been a continuous decline in resource prices for the entire century." And Nordhaus adds, "Unless all materials suddenly hit a kink in the cost curve at the same time, it seems unreasonable to foresee a drastic runup of the costs of minerals relative to wages in the near future."[6] Given continued progress in technology, a flexible price system, and adequate supplies of en-

ergy, the general conclusion must be that a shortage of industrial materials is not likely to be, at
least in the foreseeable future, one of our serious
resource problems. I shall return to the question
of energy shortly.

The report of the Paley Commission also emphasized the increasing dependence of the
United States on foreign sources of raw materials. Based on its estimates of production and
consumption of materials other than food and
gold, it found that in 1900 the United States had
a 15 percent surplus available for export, as
against a deficit of 9 percent and a prospective
deficit of 20 percent in 1975. Later investigations
of U.S. foreign trade in raw materials indicate an
interesting situation.[7] For a very small number of
materials, including platinum, mica, chromium,
and strontium, the United States is completely
dependent on foreign sources of supply. This
was true in 1950, and it is also true today. With
respect to other raw materials, the United
States—with the exception of oil, gas, iron ore,
and zinc—is not any more dependent in 1975
than it was in 1950. Imports of iron and zinc
could be replaced by domestic production and
substitution without a large increase in costs. It is
a different matter for oil and gas. The fact is that
the American raw materials trade is now heavily
influenced by oil imports and food exports. This
will have a considerable bearing on the future

energy position of the United States and on the future food situation in the rest of the world.

The Environmental Considerations

As I suggested earlier, the report of the Paley Commission is interesting not only because of its findings, but because of what it ignored. It says nothing about the desirability of protecting the environment in the course of meeting American materials requirements. One could defend the commission by saying that it was not asked to consider this question. However, a more perspicacious group of enquirers—particularly a group that emphasized the importance of real costs—might have asked themselves the question, How much will an adequate protection of the environment add to the cost of meeting materials requirements? In fact, it was not asked, and, in 1950 few, if any, were asking this question. Enquiry into the costs of environmental protection burgeoned only in the last fifteen to twenty years, and RFF has been a leader in this enquiry.

One would have to go back to the conservation movement which flourished between 1890 and 1910 in order to discover the initial impetus in this country for environmental protection. This was a political movement with objectives as disparate as saving the forests, destroying the monopolies, and maintaining Anglo-Saxon supremacy. Its economic analysis was practically nonexistent, though it did emphasize the importance of sustained yield in renewable resources. The best it could do in defining the meaning of conservation was to say that it meant a "wise use of resources." Since almost any program could be accommodated under this rubric, we can sympathize with President Taft's dictum, "A great many people are in favor of conservation no matter what it means."[8] Despite the fuzziness of the concept, however, many in the conservation movement had a feeling for environmental values of a very modern character. The American frontier was disappearing, urban congestion was increasing rapidly, the farm population had begun to decline, forests were being raped, and rivers and lakes had become polluted. No general solution to these problems existed, other than to "prevent waste," but there is no doubt that a high value was assigned to environmental protection.

The question is, How much will it cost us to maintain an adequate protection of the environment? Or, to put the query in the form in which it currently engages attention, How much of our growth rate will need to be sacrificed in order to maintain the air and water standards, the urban noise levels, and the availability of natural resources amenities that we are willing to live with? There have been some attempts to estimate, in terms of their percentages of the GNP, the costs of maintaining, particularly, certain air and water standards, but at best they are educated guesses. There are difficulties in specifying the procedures to be used in pollution abatement and estimating the costs thereof; there are difficulties in defining the objectives sought to be attained; and there are difficulties in relating the cost and benefits of pollution abatement to a meaningful measure of national income or the GNP. According to the venturesome United Nations study, *The Study of the World Economy*, directed by Leontief and others, countries with per capita incomes above $2,000 would need to spend from 1.4 to 1.9 percent of their GNP for pollution abatement to attain air, water, and waste disposal standards specified by U.S. agencies.[9] For these purposes, the United States spent 1.6 percent of its GNP in 1974, but how effective this was in attaining government-specified standards is not fully known. According to the Survey of Current Business, "In 1974 non-farm business firms spent $5.6 billion for new plant and equipment to abate air and water pollution and dispose of solid waste. . . ." This amounted to 5 percent of total new plant and equipment spending.[10] Allen V. Kneese estimates that by spending 5 percent of their GNP from now to the end of the century, "Developed countries should be able to reduce the amount of residuals discharge to their environment to a small fraction of what it is now."[11] How this small fraction would relate to U.S. standards is not indicated. Five percent would appear to be on the high side of existing estimates of expenditures needed to maintain government-specified standards. These estimates appear to converge on a figure of, perhaps, 2.5 percent during a catch-up period of a few years, followed by a reduction to, perhaps, 2 percent a year. How such expenditures would affect the GNP, as it is conventionally calculated, is unclear, but such a rate of expenditures on pollution abatement would obviously mean a considerable shift in patterns of consumption. We would consume less of some goods and services than we are accustomed to consume but would enjoy access to a purer environment. Welfare might well be improved whatever happened to GNP as conventionally calculated. The estimates we have cited presumably do not cover the costs of providing other urban and natural environmental amenities. All that we can be sure of is that there is a real conflict between the objectives of economic growth, as conventionally conceived, and protection of the environment.

It is, in fact, rather early to make overall estimates of the cost of environmental protection. The problem needs to be broken down into its constituent parts, in order to devise better measures of social costs and social benefits; and a greater effort must be made to learn how to establish a political consensus on the objectives to be reached before we attempt to strike a balance between growth and protection of the environment. There seems little doubt that this is the natural resource problem of today and the immediate future. We encounter it on every side, in the siting of electrical plants, the laying of pipelines in Alaska, the disposal of nuclear wastes, the problem of automobile emissions, the pollution of lakes and rivers, urban noise levels—one could go on indefinitely. Resources for the Future has worked effectively on many of these problems, and I would suppose this will constitute its central activity for a long time to come.

The Myth of Scarcity

Despite the dicta of the Club of Rome, we are not facing scarcities of industrial materials. So far as I can see, we do not even confront a danger of rising costs of these materials for the next century at least, and probably longer. On the world scene, the principal scarcity problem is finding enough food to feed a continuously expanding population, and, indeed, if there are no limits to population growth, it may be an insoluble problem. I see no serious scarcity problems for the United States as a whole, assuming that we can adopt a sensible energy policy.

Edward S. Mason

A striking feature of the energy situation in the United States is that while we are confronted with impending shortages of such highly convenient energy sources as oil and gas, there are not practical limits to alternative supplies—coal, nuclear power, and, with improved technology, other sources—which can be made available over time and perhaps at no considerable increase in real costs. At present rates of consumption and using known technologies, it is probably true that the United States and the world, despite additional discoveries, will run out of oil and gas early in the twenty-first century. If consumption continues to increase at the 1970's rate of 6 percent per annum, exhaustion of available supplies that can be made available with existing technology, and at something like the present price, would come sooner. Exhaustion, however, will not take place at a precise date, with ample supplies before that date and zero supplies afterwards. Instead it is likely to be a protracted process, with rising prices shutting off certain areas of consumption. It should not be beyond the wit of man to prolong the availability of gas and oil by confining their use by strict economies to areas in which there are no convenient substitutes. Unimpeded market forces would, in the course of time, accomplish this purpose, but the process could be facilitated by governmental action, including differential taxation of the uses that need to be discouraged.

This is to view the situation from the demand side and over the relatively short run. In the long run it is possible that improved technology can make available at something like current real prices the very large quantities of natural liquid and gaseous hydrocarbons that are known to be below the surface of the earth. It is possible. But, until more is known of these potentialities, a sensible energy policy must primarily emphasize economizing on supplies that are amenable to conventional methods of extraction.

When oil prices were quadrupled in 1973 because of OPEC, the world, including the United States, took a large, and probably irreversible step away from low-cost energy toward a condition in which energy prices will be persistently higher. In the United States the full effects of that step, however, are not as yet worked out. Government controls still maintain a distinction between old and new oil, and natural gas is still being sold in producing states at prices substantially higher than gas being sold for interstate shipment. This situation cannot last for long. President Carter's energy proposals, if accepted, will eliminate some of these anomalies and, even without government action, market forces within a few years could bring the prices of energy from different sources into some kind of equilibrium. This equilibrated system of prices will provide energy in the United States and elsewhere at a substantially higher cost than pre-1973 costs.

But, given time to bring energy sources other than oil and gas into effective production, it may well be at costs that need not be subject to further substantial increases. Assuming that we can bridge the time gap involved in developing these sources, without falling prey to an attempt by OPEC to maximize its short-run monopoly profits, the price of oil is likely over time to move at levels close to the costs of alternative sources of energy. The money price of oil will presumably continue to increase along with inflation in the prices of other goods.

But the real cost of energy to the United States will depend on the cost of expanding coal production, the cost of increasing nuclear energy with existing technology, and the costs of developing energy from other sources with improved technology. There will, of course, be manifold adaptations in use, as well as in production processes, but, so far as I can see, there need not be very large increases in the average real cost of different energy resources for the United States. What happens to energy costs, of course, will be an important determinant of the real costs of other materials, since the extraction of metals from leaner ore bodies and the recycling of materials substantially increases demand for energy.

The fact that the United States as a whole does not, in my view, confront serious scarcity problems should not be taken to mean that particular regions do not confront such shortages. Clearly, the principal one is the shortage of water in the Southwest and the High Plains. It should be obvious by now that the limits for irrigated agriculture in the West and Southwest have been reached, if not passed, and that if the growing cities of the area are to have enough water, it will have to be at the expense of local agriculture. A proper pricing of water could do much to accomplish this objective, while a sensible recycling of water can substantially increase its availability. Local shortages have always affected the location of industry and population. Heavy water-using industries cannot be sited in areas without streams, and citrus fruits cannot be grown in the Rocky Mountains; but this does not mean that the nation's resources cannot provide adequate food, clothing, and housing for its population into the indefinite future. The fact that not everybody can live in the Sun Belt can hardly be said to constitute a natural resource limitation to national growth.

The Real Issues of Externalities

In the natural resource area the shift away from problems of scarcity toward the interrelation between growth and the protection of the environment has led to new developments in economic and political analysis. In economics, the concepts of public goods and externalities have been brought out of the cupboard and subjected to renewed scrutiny. In politics, the problem of achieving at least a practical course of action, if not consensus, in an area beset with conflicting interests and discordant values, has taken on new dimensions.

The concept of public goods is at least as old as the science of economics. In Adam Smith's time the emphasis was on the economies of scale, which dictated that the provision of certain goods and services lay beyond the capacity of private enterprise and must therefore be undertaken by the state. The services of defense had to be provided on a national scale; making roadways, sewage facilities, and parks available to all on a community basis was much cheaper than to provide these facilities to each household privately. The surrounding atmosphere did not come into the discussion as a public good, and nobody talked about the ecosphere, the biosphere, or any other kind of sphere.

Although economies of scale still have relevance for certain types of public goods, primary attention has shifted to the problem of congestion. No one can be excluded from the use of public good because it is impossible to charge a price for the use of the goods or because it is socially undesirable to do so. Although Samuelson defines pure public goods as goods for which additional consumption by one individual does not diminish the amount available to others,[12] not many public goods are "pure." In fact, national defense may be one of the few examples. A more typical example of a public good is a public highway on which, at least during rush hours, additional use by one or more individuals definitely seems to diminish the space available to others. Or, to take another example, the use of a stream by a pulp mill will certainly diminish the downstream access to pure water. Most of the problems of environmental protection arise from the impossibility of excluding other users of the parks, public beaches, and other so-called public amenities.

As Rothenberg observes, "Depending on the nature of the public good, a differing but rather wide range of users may be accommodated with no perceivable deterioration of quality. Each good has a capacity or threshold." [13] Beyond that, quality deteriorates with increasing congestion. Pollution is a particular form of congestion in which the users are divided into those who pollute and those who are the victims of pollution. The current analysis of public goods centers on these various consequences of congestion.

The other ancient concept that has been resurrected and put to new uses by the emergence of environmental problems is that of "externalities." An external effect occurs when the costs or benefits of an activity are not limited to the individual or firm responsible for it but are shared by outsiders. The early discussion of externalities concentrated, for some reason or another, on bucolic examples. The bees of farmer A collect honey from the flowers of farmer B, with subsequent loss to farmer B; lumbering operations on a hillside lead to excessive runoffs and floods, damaging properties in the valley; cinders from locomotives set fire to adjacent wheat fields; or straying cattle trample crops on other people's land. These stories of the birds and bees, formerly thought useful in conveying the facts of life to our children, seem to have seized the imagination of nineteenth-century writers on externalities. When Milton Friedman lumps the whole problem of externalities under the innocuous phrase "neighborhood effects," he seems to be thinking in much the same way.[14]

When one looks, however, at the extensive pollution of air and water resources, interference in the radio spectrum, and the struggles in the West for access to public lands and public waters, it is difficult to sweep the problems of externalities that are involved under the rug of "neighborhood effects." We are accustomed in our youth, or at least I was, in our reading and at the movies, to learn about the struggles between sheepmen and cattlemen for access to public grazing lands. This conflict was an early example of congestion, or is it pollution? These struggles pale, however, before the cutthroat competition for scarce water in the West. Public goods and externalities are at the heart of the problem. Again, RFF has been at the forefront in exploring the modern applications of these concepts.

Environmental concerns have also greatly extended the dimensions of political analysis. If the primary concern of politics is who gets what, when, where, and how, one welcomes an opportunity to analyze the process of sharing environmental resources and amenities among competing interest groups, or states, or communities concerned with employment or economic growth. There is little doubt that adequate protection of the environment will markedly increase the role of government in society and test the ability of representative government to achieve a workable concensus of conflicting claims of growth and environmental protection and to devise efficient procedures to implement this concensus. This does not mean that all the advantages of the impersonal market need be thrown away. Indeed, one of the advantageous ways of dealing with certain types of environmental protection is through pollution charges, leaving the polluter a certain measure of freedom in the choice of ways and means. But, even here, it will have to be the government that assesses the requirements and fixes the charges, while the most serious issues involved in choices between growth and environmental protection will have to be decided, not in the market, but in the political arena.

What is now happening in the world suggests that natural resource problems, including possible conflicts between growth and protection of the environment, raise issues not limited to the United States or any other single country. Smoke emitted from high stacks in Britain comes down as acid rain in Norway; in their pursuit of whales, Japan and the Soviet Union may rid the world of these interesting mammals. Tuna fishermen are decimating our stock of dolphins. The potential mineral resources of the seabed are a current source of fierce international debate. The uneven spread of arable land and mineral resources across the surface of the earth creates opportunities for international trade and investment that need to be sensibly exploited if the benefits of growth are to be widely shared. Resources for the Future has begun to explore a number of these areas and is likely to find, in the course of these explorations, plenty of problems to engage its attention in the next quarter-century.

Footnotes

[1] This conclusion and the following figures are taken from E. S. Mason, "American Security and Access to Raw Materials," *World Politics* (January 1949), p. 148.

[2] In addition to the above-mentioned article, see E. S. Mason, "Raw Materials, Rearmament and Economic Development," *Quarterly Journal of Economics* (August 1952); and "An American View of Raw Materials," *Journal of Industrial Economics* (November 1952).

[3] President's Materials Policy Committee, *Resources for Freedom*, vol. 1 (Washington, GPO, 1952), p. 12.

[4] A principal finding of the Paley Commission report (President's Materials Policy Committee, vol. I, p. 4), was that "the value of the material stream rose by only half as much as the national output; (1900–1950) services were beginning to become a larger proportion of the goods and services that made up this output, and more value was being added to materials by successively higher fabrication as time went on."

[5] H. J. Barnett and C. Morse, *Scarcity and Growth; the Economics of Natural Resource Availability* (Baltimore, Johns Hopkins University Press for Resources for the Future, 1962), p. 233. Workers in extractive industries (including agriculture) as a percentage of all U.S. workers declined from 52 percent in 1870 to 11 percent in 1957. Barnett later reexamined this proposition, bringing the calculations of materials cost up to 1970 (*Scarcity and Growth Revisited*—Mimeograph, 1972). He found that, in general, the record of declining costs continues.

[6] W. D. Nordhaus, "Resources as Constraints on Growth," *American Economic Review* (May 1974), p. 24.

[7] Compare with H. Landsberg, "Energy and Materials; How They Differ in the International Context," *Engineering and Mining Journal*, vol. 177, no. 10 (October 1976), pp. 63–71. RFF Reprint 135, 1976.

[8] *Outlook* (May 14, 1910), p. 57.

[9] United Nations, *The Future of the World Economy* (Preliminary report, 1976), pp. 29–30.

[10] *Survey of Current Business* (July 1975), p. 15.

[11] A. V. Kneese, *Economics and Environment* (Baltimore, Penguin Books, 1977), p. 252.

[12] P. A. Samuelson, "The Pure Theory of Public Expenditures," *Review of Economics and Statistics* (November 1954).

Edward S. Mason

[13] J. Rothenberg, "The Economics of Congestion and Pollution: An Integrated View," *American Economic Review*, vol. 9, no. 2, p. 14.

[14] M. Friedman, "The Role of Government: Neighborhood Effects," reprinted in R. and N. Dorfman, *Economics of the Government* (New York, Norton, 1972), p. 202.

Resources and Environment in the Next Quarter-Century

Harrison Brown

Director, Resource Systems Institute, East–West Center, and Member of the Board of Directors of Resources for the Future

Before speculating about what the next twenty-five years might have in store for us, it is of some importance to examine the major concerns about resources which were relevant twenty-five years ago and compare them with those of today.

Yesterday

Resources for the Future was born in an atmosphere of technological optimism. In spite of the Korean War, which had recently been concluded, there was also a great deal of optimism concerning America's position in the world and the state of the American economy. Thanks in part to the Marshall Plan the economies of Europe and Japan were recovering rapidly. The cold war was in full swing, and defense industries were booming. There seemed little doubt that the Soviet Union would be contained militarily regardless of her nuclear capacity. The level of affluence in the United States was unprecedented and growing rapidly. Never before had a large population of human beings been so well off.

Attitudes concerning nonrenewable resources can be judged by the thinking at the time concerning energy, the "ultimate resource." I remember attending a conference at Northwestern University in early 1951 on the subject of world population and future resources. Great concern was expressed at the conference about population growth, but little alarm was expressed about future supplies of energy, despite the fact that the United States had crossed the line only three or four years earlier to become a net importer of liquid fuels.

Robert E. Wilson, then chairman of the board of the Standard Oil Company of Indiana, spoke eloquently on this subject.[1] His main conclusion was that "America can continue to have plentiful supplies of liquid fuels at reasonable cost for many generations to come if she will do just three things, namely, preserve freedom of enterprise, freedom of research, and adequate incentives." He recognized that U.S. fuel requirements could not be met indefinitely from domestic crude oil resources and suggested, with considerable confidence, that we could probably turn first "to imported petroleum; second, to natural gas; third, to oil shale; fourth, to coal; fifth, to tar sands; sixth, to agricultural products; and seventh, to air, water, and sunlight." He placed great stress upon the future importance of imports and emphasized that, fortunately, "the great bulk of all Western

Hemisphere reserves and about half of the probable Near East reserves are in American control." He expanded the view that the trend toward imports is "a healthy development, but the healthiest thing about it is that natural economic conditions determine it, and not someone else's ideas of what should be done." Wilson was not specific as to what he meant by "natural economic conditions," nor did he suggest that such conditions might be related to the fact that Middle Eastern oil was selling for $1.50 a barrel at a time when the incremental cost of the oil at dockside was about $0.10 a barrel. He did say, however, that "the richness of some of the Middle East resources is not widely appreciated."

The report of the Paley Commission appeared in 1952, and it, too, was generally optimistic about the future of oil and of energy. The report stressed that it would be prudent for us to import relatively low-cost oil, thus saving our own. There was no implication that there would be a supply problem in the near future, stressing that "there is as yet no evidence of failure to discover resources adequate to support growing production."[2]

There were, of course, some individuals who were less optimistic; for example, M. King Hubbert, who had published his classic paper, "Energy from Fossil Fuels," in 1949.[3] Application of the principles which he enunciated suggested that crude oil production in the conterminous

27

United States might well peak about 1970. But even this possibility gave little cause for alarm. Quite apart from the availability for import of huge quantities of inexpensive crude oil in South America and the Middle East, we knew that the United States was endowed with vast quantities of coal and oil shale, which our technological prowess would enable us to convert to liquid fuels. Furthermore, we were confident that electricity generated from nuclear energy was very close to being economically practicable. There appeared to be little need to worry.

At the Mid-Century Conference on Resources, which was sponsored by Resources for the Future in 1953, experts divided sharply into two groups. The larger group was composed of the technological optimists—who their protagonists dubbed "cornucopians." The smaller group was composed of those who held strong conservationist views and who sincerely believed that our rapidly expanding consumption of nonrenewable resources was leading industrial societies, and the world, toward disaster. Now, twenty-five years later, we realize that in many ways both groups were right—and that they were, in a sense, arguing about the wrong problems.

The conservationists of twenty-five years ago were the forerunners—indeed, one might say the founders—of today's school of thought concerning the limits to growth. In 1953 Samuel Ordway,

Jr., in his *Resources and the American Dream*,[4] summarized the views of this group as follows:

> Levels of human living are constantly rising with mounting use of natural resources.
>
> Despite technological progress we are spending each year more resource capital than is created.
>
> If this cycle continues long enough, basic resources will come into such short supply that rising costs will make their use in additional production unprofitable, industrial expansion will cease, and we shall have reached the limit of growth.

It is interesting to note that in this great cornucopian—conservationist debate there was no mention of the possible global environmental consequences of human actions, with the single exception of the effects of improper land use.

Today

A quarter of a century has now passed, and in that period we have seen the U.S. resource position change in dramatic ways that had not been foreseen. As had been anticipated by some persons, proved reserves of crude oil in the conterminous United States peaked about 1960, and production peaked about 1970. Although the Paley Commission forecasts for total U.S. petroleum demand in 1975 were remarkably accurate, the estimate of total U.S. production turned out to be high by one-third, and the estimate of imports was low by a factor of between two and three. All signs now point to a continued rapid growth in U.S. dependence upon imports of crude oil.

At the same time, there has been a widening cleavage between the rich and the poor countries brought about, in part, by rapid growth of affluence in the rich ones and rapid population growth in the poor. Most reserves of exportable crude oil are found in developing countries. These countries also possess large reserves of nonfuel minerals which the industrial nations need.

With the proliferation of politically independent national states which take their so-called sovereignty extremely seriously, and with the emergence of OPEC as an effective cartel, the "American control," which was referred to rather confidently by Robert E. Wilson, has in large measure disappeared. Further, there has emerged within the developing countries a deep-seated and increasingly militant antagonism toward the rich ones.

In 1973–74 the industrial democracies reeled from a shockwave: first, the fourfold increase in the price of crude oil imposed by the Organization of Petroleum Exporting Countries (OPEC); and then, the Arab oil embargo. In a brief, three-month period we saw wave after wave sweep through our economies. Even more important, we saw control of access to crude oil used for the first time as a major weapon of war. Almost instantaneously,

Japan did an about-face in her foreign policy with respect to Israel. Western Europe was severely shaken. Great Britain was particularly hard hit, because the embargo began when considerable disruption had occurred as the result of strikes by electrical workers and coal miners.

During and shortly after the crisis of 1973–74, there was much talk about the United States achieving greater energy independence. Now, only four years later, after hearing much talk and seeing almost no action, we appear to be even further from that goal than we were then. We now import well over half of the petroleum we need in the form of crude oil and refined petroleum products. As a result of this, we are running balance-of-payments deficits of unprecedented size. These are increasing despite our efforts to export increasing quantities of agricultural and industrial products and despite the fact that we have greatly expanded exports of expensive sophisticated weaponry—particularly to major oil exporters—with potentially disastrous consequences for world peace.

Major oil exporters have been saving or investing substantial shares of their oil earnings in the United States. Much of the money which has been deposited in U.S. banks has been loaned to Third World countries, enabling them to pay their oil import bills. Nevertheless, there is now considerable danger of defaults on a large scale.

The other industrial democracies currently find themselves in an even more difficult position than does the United States, for they must import even greater amounts of their crude oil. In order to pay for their increased imports, they, too, must export more. As in the United States, these export drives have led to expanded weapons sales, as well as to sales of dangerous nuclear technologies and a major resurgence of protectionism.

At the same time, the tensions between the industrial democracies and the poor nations are increasing in substantial measure because of the rich countries' control of production, investment, and trade. The developing countries seek agreements involving their trade position with respect to about a dozen major commodities, excluding oil, which account for about 80 percent of their export earnings. They demand a higher proportion of the consumer price, and they would like to establish a mechanism for eliminating disastrous price fluctuations. Beyond commodities, they would like to see major relaxation of present restrictions against importation of their manufactured products. They, too, must export in order to pay for their petroleum imports.

In this struggle between the rich and poor nations, OPEC is, for understandable reasons, championing the cause of the poor and is in a position to use two major weapons—oil and money—to achieve this and related goals.

As the struggle goes on, the Soviet Union can afford to wait it out for she is basically self-sufficient with respect to resources. This is an overwhelming geopolitical fact—the ultimate significance of which few of us fully appreciate. To be sure, the Soviet Union has some technical and organizational problems in tapping her considerable oil and gas reservoirs and developing adequate distribution systems from remote areas. But it seems likely that she will solve these problems, while making full use of her unequaled coal reserves. At the same time, she is exporting substantial quantities of petroleum and gas to her energy-poor satellites in Eastern Europe. This, of course, provides her with an element of political control which transcends armies in its power.

Why is it, that in spite of our vast resources of coal and oil shale, our nuclear technology, and our potential for utilizing solar energy, we have not been able to halt the increasing need for petroleum imports? In substantial measure this stems from the incredible inexpensiveness of crude oil and natural gas, as they are priced today. Nothing else can really compete. All alternative energy options require tremendous capital investments, and even when the economics are favorable, a great deal of time is required to reduce new approaches to practicality. Added to this, virtually all possibilities for large-scale power generation have environmental problems associated with them, most of which are probably solvable but costly in both money and time. Further, a mystique has arisen concerning nuclear power which makes it increasingly difficult to build new plants or to operate old ones.

The fact is that we have become "hooked" on crude oil and natural gas and the cost of kicking the habit is substantial.

Tomorrow

The problems that will confront us during the next twenty-five years are clearly formidable. The greatest likelihood is that we will continue on our present course and that the needs of the industrial democracies for imported crude oil will continue to increase. The evidence suggests that world production of crude oil is likely to peak around the year 2000, and a major question will be whether we will be able to cope with this situation, which is not so very far in the future.

But quite apart from our ability to cope with the problem of the beginning of the end of crude oil, we will be called upon to handle a multiplicity of other energy-related problems long before that time. Crude oil is now a recognized weapon of war, no matter whether it will be directed by the Arab states against Japan or the United States for their policies with respect to Israel, or by the United Nations against South Africa for its social policies.

It is of great importance that we recognize fully the vulnerability of the United States, Western Europe, and Japan to major disruptions in the flow of crude oil. We can be destroyed more effectively, and certainly much more neatly in this way, than were we at the receiving end of a massive H-bomb attack. Indeed, the dedicated use of the oil weapon could kill us as a functioning nation. The possibility of its use could lead us to take actions which might be equally disastrous. In my opinion, the United States is in a far more dangerous position today than at any time since the Civil War. Japan and Western Europe are in even more dangerous positions.

Thus, I believe it is essential that the industrial democracies diversify their sources of energy as quickly as possible. This will not be easy because no matter what route is taken, the costs of energy will go up. In particular, capital costs will become very large.

Unfortunately, this is a problem which simply cannot be solved through the free movement of market forces, which would lead simply to continued rapid increases of imports, further increasing our vulnerability. The situation is one in which government must intervene, providing needed incentives and disincentives, as well as guarantees.

How much should we be willing to pay for energy? Are the present economics of energy really functioning for long-term human benefit when such economics make it so attractive for us to consume the greater part of the existing petroleum and natural gas in the world before we learn how to use coal and oil shale effectively?

Clearly, the fairness of a price should be related in some way to the cost of doing business in the absence of the resource. If there were no crude oil available, hydrocarbon fuels would be obtained by conversion of oil shale or coal to synthetic fuels. If the price of crude oil were raised to a level greater than the cost of converting oil shale or coal, and if the price were predictably maintained, there would be little question that conversion plants would be built in profusion.

Of course, when the price of crude oil was raised so rapidly in 1973–74, the consumer nations could not have taken any meaningful action for the simple reason that options other than that of accepting the increased prices (or perhaps engaging in military action) were simply not viable. A great deal of time is required to develop the necessary technology, to accumulate the needed substantial capital, and to build the plants.

If energy sources other than crude oil and natural gas are to be developed and put into operation on a meaningful scale for the generation of power and the production of liquid fuels, the price structure of our various energy resources must be reexamined and drastically altered. Here,

I use the term *price* to include all costs to the consumer including taxes, less government subsidies.

Ideally, the revised price structure and associated guarantees would make oil shale and coal competitive with crude oil and natural gas (both domestic and imported) for the production of liquid fuels and petrochemicals. Nuclear power from fission would be made competitive with coal for the generation of electricity. Solar energy would be made competitive with fossil fuels for space heating and cooling. In this way, all of our major, near-term energy possibilities would be developed and utilized on a substantial scale.

Of course, under such circumstances our energy costs would be greater than they are today, but probably not more than double the current price of imported crude oil. And here we must keep in mind that, even if we do nothing, the price will at least double again anyway as the result of outside forces. How much better it would be for the increases to be under our own control, and on a schedule developed by us!

It is essential that the importing industrial nations—Japan, the nations of Western Europe, and the United States—arrive at a common agreement on energy pricing and on taking artificially higher energy costs into account in the pricing of their manufactured and agricultural products, particularly those for export. To take an extreme case, were Japan to continue with OPEC oil as its primary source of energy, and were Germany to shift primarily to coal and nuclear energy, Japan would, for the time being, have a marked economic advantage. Obviously, some compensatory understanding would be necessary to keep the system from falling apart.

No matter how we handle our energy problems during the next twenty-five years, we must face the fact that the environmental element of the energy equation will become increasingly important. It is difficult to see how reasonable levels of energy self-sufficiency can be achieved in the near term unless nuclear energy is used on a substantial scale, and the environmental problems that would be associated with this are well known. Unfortunately, the mystique which has arisen in most industrial nations concerning the dangers associated with nuclear power has taken on the appearance of a religious war, in which logic and experience have been lost sight of and actions are governed largely by emotions. Reasonableness will not be brought back into the nuclear power picture unless rules are adopted for nuclear power plant siting and generating procedures. It must be made obvious to everyone that accidents which can endanger human life will be rare; large-scale human catastrophe will be virtually impossible; radioactive wastes can be stored safely; and diversion of explosive-grade nuclear materials will be so difficult that it will not be a matter of serious concern. I believe that these goals are technologically and administratively feasible.

Finally, during the next twenty-five years we must come to grips seriously with the problem of the increasing carbon dioxide content of the atmosphere. I suspect that sooner or later it will become necessary for nations to limit their rates of combustion of fossil fuels. This would mean converting to a combination of nuclear and solar power. From a technological point of view, this would certainly be feasible. But in a multinational world, in which each nation guards its sovereignty, how would the rationing of fossil fuel combustion be accomplished?

Indeed, if I were asked to identify the greatest single barrier to the solutions of global resource, environmental, and development problems in the world today, I would necessarily point to the tight grip in which the concept of national sovereignty holds the world's peoples. I suspect that at least another century must pass before this force is no longer dominant. Under the circumstances, we in the United States must come to grips with our resources problems on the assumption that, for some time in the future, we will continue to be a part of an anarchic world.

I have confined my discussion to energy because, given adequate supplies of energy, we need never suffer from lack of nonfuel minerals. I have confined my discussion of energy to those aspects of energy which will be of greatest importance during the next twenty-five years.

We must face the fact that we are living in a period marked by the convergence of several critical trends. In addition to energy, these include growing affluence and population, diminishing resources, expanding weaponry, and the increasing tensions between the rich and poor nations. The time scale for this convergence is about another twenty-five years. If by that time we have not truly come to grips with these problems in a significant way, we will find ourselves in the middle of a crunch to end all crunches.

The way in which we navigate the next twenty-five years will be crucial for the survival of our civilization. The obstacles in our path are numerous and will be difficult to overcome. I am convinced, however, that those obstacles can be overcome and that we can create a new and higher level of civilization. We certainly have it in our power to do so. The real question is, Do we have the political will?

Footnotes

[1]P. K. Hatt, ed. *World Population and Future Resources* (New York, American Book Company, 1952) pp. 212–228.

[2]Report of the President's Materials Policy Commission. *The Outlook for Energy Resources,* vol. III (Washington, G.P.O., 1952) p. 5.

[3]M. K. Hubbert, "Energy from Fossil Fuels," *Science* vol. 109 (1949) pp. 103–109.

[4]S. H. Ordway, Jr. *Resources and the American Dream* (New York, Ronald Press, 1953).

Energy Imperatives and the Environment

Robert W. Fri

Former Deputy Administrator of the Environmental Protection
Agency and the Energy Research and Development Administration

Energy and environment is a common enough
juxtaposition. In fact, it is rather old hat. But why
should I speak of energy *imperatives*? What is
imperative about energy? And why not *environmental* imperatives?

To get a handle on this title, let me first examine the nature of the energy problem and its impact on the environment, and then turn to the
central issue that the energy–environment trade-off seems to raise. It is, I believe, an institutional
issue rather than a technical one.

The Energy Imperative

The energy problem is hard to understand without looking ahead at least twenty or thirty years.
Regrettably, few thorough studies of the problem
with this time horizon have been published. As a
result, I am going to rely on an unpublished study,
the Market-Oriented Program Planning Study
(MOPPS), undertaken by an extinct Energy Research and Development Administration (ERDA).

Robert W. Fri

It has been, as some of you know, a controversial work. However, I believe it is a thorough, detailed, and balanced analysis and will prove to be a significant contribution to our understanding of our energy situation.

The central point that MOPPS makes is that we do not have a long-term energy shortage, but that we do have an awesome transitional problem —especially in liquid fuels.

Between now and the year 2000, adequate liquid fuel supplies—especially for transportation fuels and petrochemical feedstocks—persist as the central energy problem. Under the National Energy Plan (NEP) ground rules, as originally proposed by President Carter, MOPPS projects that oil imports would amount to 14.2 quads in 1985 and 10.5 quads by 2000. These levels, representing 40 percent of our oil consumption in 1985 and 33 percent in the year 2000, indicate a continuing high dependence on imported petroleum.

But even this relatively high import level may be too optimistic, because the forces driving up the demand for liquid fuels by the year 2000 are hard to resist and may push the demand higher than even MOPPS projects. Transportation is one such force. The demand for gasoline and diesel fuel is likely to rise sharply after 2000, if not before, because, by then, increases in miles driven simply overwhelm all our efforts at conservation. MOPPS projects a 30 percent increase in demand for these fuels between the years 2000 and 2010. Of course, this sharp rise could occur earlier.

Another such driving force is the demand for petrochemical feedstocks. Feedstocks necessarily rise with industrial growth, going from 7.8 quads in 1985 to 11.5 quads in 2000. Within this 50 percent overall growth, liquid demand triples. In principle, natural gas could substitute for liquid fuels as a feedstock. But, owing to gas shortages today, industry is turning increasingly to liquid fuels. As a result, the substitution will be deferred, and liquid fuel demand will stay high.

A final force behind the liquid fuel demand is old housing in the Northeast, where both fuel switching and meaningful conservation measures are exceedingly difficult to achieve.

These forces suggest, if anything, a continuing higher demand for liquid fuels. But even if we cope successfully with such forces, other events could exacerbate our problem. If, for example, electricity demand does not slow markedly from historical rates, industry fails to convert to coal, or our conservation efforts falter, we must turn at least in part to liquid fuels to take up the slack.

Thus, the odds are quite high that the liquids problem will be worse than what the aggregate figures show. It would not be unreasonable to expect added liquid fuel import deficits of 1.5 quads in 1985 and 10 quads in 2000. In case of such deficits, imports would rise to 42 percent of our total oil demand in 1985 and to 49 percent in 2000. These figures, incidentally, are consistent with those projected by the excellent report of the Workshop on Alternative Energy Strategies (WAES).

What about our other energy supplies? Coal certainly presents a more tractable problem than liquid fuels, simply because we have lots of it. The problem here centers around the ability of the market to absorb more coal, even though there are serious questions about our ability to mine it in the first place. Between 1978 and 2000, the utilities' consumption of coal may rise from 8.8 to 20 quads—a large but attainable increase. Industrial use, on the other hand, must quadruple—from 3.7 to 15.8 quads. This is a formidable, and perhaps unattainable, target.

Nuclear power shows similarly large growth rates—assuming the uranium is there. Nuclear power now generates 1.9 quads of energy, and by 2000 should produce nearly 20 quads if the pressures on coal mining are to be kept in bounds. To reach this target, however, nuclear power would have to capture 60 percent of the new power plant market, and that is far higher than its current penetration.

Gas is, interestingly enough, less of a problem. Although we have curtailments today, our natural gas resources are very large, if we are willing to pay the price to top them. Indeed, at a price we can obtain immense sources of gas from coal, the geopressurized zone, or other exotic sources. The problem we face here is one of timing. MOPPS estimates that, in 1985, our gas supply could run anywhere from 3 quads short to 6 quads long. By 2000, the deficit could be 6 quads, and the surplus could be 12 quads. The actual figure depends on how fast we move to free up our gas resources. Thus, with natural gas, the problem is less one of adequate resources than of near-term producibility.

Exotic energy sources—solar, geothermal, and the like—will produce significant energy by the end of the century. MOPPS estimates 0.5 quads in 1985 and 3.8 quads in 2000. Yet, even in 2000, this amount accounts only for 3 percent of total demand. The prospect is encouraging, but falls short of being our energy salvation.

Finally, there is conservation. The total demand for energy in MOPPS is 94 quads in 1985 and 118 quads in 2000. These levels are quite low, lower than those of the NEP, in fact, and they represent savings of 15 or 20 percent over business as usual. However, the failure of this aggressive conservation program has serious consequences. Failure in the industrial sector puts enormous strains on coal use, and in the transportation sector, on liquid fuels. Neither problem is affordable.

Earlier, I said that we do not have an energy shortage. Having just enumerated several energy problems that certainly sound like shortages, let me explain what I mean. I think that the energy imperative can be boiled down to these propositions:

- First, we are running out of oil, and that is a serious problem. But we have vast resources of shale, and of coal for liquefaction. It is imperative to use them.
- Second, we have large coal resources and large potential markets for them. It is imperative to make those markets real. The same can be said of nuclear resources.
- Third, natural gas is not a dying industry, but one in transition to a plentiful, but much higher-cost product. It is imperative that both the resource and economic transition be made as quickly and as painlessly as possible.
- Fourth, conservation is imperative, period.

The Environmental Response

So much for the energy imperative, what now of the environment? Fortunately, there is a recent environmental analysis of the NEP done by ERDA that allows us to be fairly precise about the environmental response to the energy imperative. And there is good news and bad news.

There is good news of a sort, anyhow; the situation is not so bad as you might think. For example, the report projects that all air pollutants will increase somewhat between 1985 and 2000 but suggests that three of five criteria pollutants will remain well below 1975 levels. Similarly, four of five major water pollutants will drop significantly from 1975 to 2000, with suspended solids dropping by 88 percent.

And energy becomes less of a factor in the overall pollution control problem. Generally, pollution control costs will drop from 2.1 to 1.1 percent of the GNP by 2000. And the energy component will drop even more sharply, from 43 percent to 31 percent of the total.

In short, the environmental impact of the NEP is not so bad. And I could end my comments at this point if it were not for two things:

● The NEP does not solve the energy problem, and, if it did, its environmental impacts would be large.

● It is the NEP's reliance on coal that is the source of all the bad news in ERDA's environmental report.

Let me take up the coal question first. Coal is the dominant source of the pollutants that do not decrease. The ERDA report estimates that, even with best available control technology (BACT), emissions of sulfur oxides in the year 2000 will exceed the 1975 levels by 20 percent, and coal combustion is the source of 80 percent of these emissions. Nitrogen oxide emissions will rise 70 percent above 1975 levels, with coal contributing 40 percent of these emissions. In water, total dissolved solids will increase by about 7 percent; in 1975 coal contributed 26 percent of this pollutant but will produce 42 percent in 2000.

However, pollution is only one type of environmental insult. Energy use of land will rise to over 10 million acres by the year 2000, 94 percent of which will be due to coal production. Depending on the region of the country, this represents from 0.5 percent to 3.6 percent of the total land area. Solid wastes, mostly from coal, will rise from the current rate of 100 million tons to over 700 million tons by 2000. And water use for energy will increase from 2 million to 11 million acre-feet per year. Energy use of water rises from 2 percent to 10 percent of our total consumption, and after the year 2000, it will only get worse.

Thus, the use of coal, as envisioned by the NEP, has serious environmental impacts. But worse, the NEP is a limited plan. By looking only as far as 1985, it does not solve the energy problem—nor, for that matter, does it expose its true magnitude. And when we look to the end of the century, it is easy to see that the energy solution requires us to rely on two environmentally intrusive resources—shale and even greater amounts of coal.

I have already mentioned the effects of relying on coal, but shale is a new story. Each quad of shale produces 37,000 tons of sulfur oxide, 140 millions tons of solid waste, and the process uses 37,000 acre-feet of water. We need 10 to 15 quads of liquid fuels to close our import gap. As a percentage of national figures, the airborne emissions and water use connected with shale oil production is small, but that of solid wastes is enormous. Unfortunately, all this impact is not national—it occurs in two counties in Colorado and a couple in Utah.

Indeed, the energy insult on the environment is highly regional. The big loser, as we all know, is the Rocky Mountain region. Under the NEP, this region receives a disproportionate share of strip-mining, mine drainage, suspended-solids runoff, solid waste production, water consumption, energy-dedicated land use, and sulfur oxide production. Thus, we cannot conclude that the NEP or MOPPS, or any other energy projection is environmentally benign.

The Tradeoff

I am afraid that I have taken you on a rather breathless tour of some new statistics. But from it all, a couple of central conclusions emerge. First, it seems clear to me that we risk exhausting our environmental resource long before we will exhaust our energy resource, unless we begin to act differently. We cannot really allow the pollutants most dangerous to our health—sulfur, nitrogen oxides, and dissolved chemicals—to persist above today's levels. Already, our air and water resources have been effectively exhausted by these pollutants. Nor can we risk the land and water use of an ever-expanding energy industry.

Second, we can conclude, I think, that energy is an imperative—or at least more of an imperative than is our environment. The forces responsible for the energy imperative are some of our most cherished national goals. It is not greed that causes our liquid fuels problem, but respectable economic growth, the inexorable growth of even energy-conservative transportation, and the age of our residences. Coal is needed for even modest industrial growth and electricity production. We must promote conservation, but not so fiercely as to slow economic growth markedly. We must not fall into the trap of saying, "Pull in the gangplank, I'm already aboard."

And so there is a conflict, a profound one. And the real issue is, How do we equip ourselves to manage this conflict for the balance of this century? What policies, and, more important, what processes and institutions must we build to carry us into the twenty-first century if we are not to exhaust our environment as we exploit our nearly inexhaustible energy resources?

I do not pretend to have the answer. But I am persuaded that the policies, processes, and institutions of today are strikingly ill-suited to provide the answer. Let me give you a few examples.

First, our energy policy simply lacks the breadth of view to resolve the energy problem compatibly with the protection of the environment. The NEP, even before it ran into congressional headwinds, looked only as far as 1985. Any plans so short-sighted cannot come to grips with the central issues of either energy or the environment. A good example of this is found in the ERDA environmental report as it deals with air pollution. Calculating air pollution loads for the NEP, and for BACT without the NEP, the loads are essentially the same. In other words, the NEP does not make any environmental difference. An energy plan that does not improve the environment is not much of a plan.

Had we an energy policy that truly addressed the environmental problem, we would have more than the energy-economic policy we have. We might have seen an aggressive program to introduce clean, coal-burning technologies—such as fuel cells, solvent-refined coal, fluidized bed combustion, and the like. We might have seen more emphasis on shale oil production *in situ,* which produces desperately needed oil in a more environmentally acceptable way than does above-ground retorting. We might even have seen a turn to coal gasification, both to firm up the long-term gas supply and to give us a way of using coal more cleanly than by direct combustion.

Of course, if we had done these things, we would have paid a price—both in development costs and in the incentives necessary to promote the commercial use of environmentally acceptable technology. But internalizing environmental costs is always expensive, and, in my judgment, always right.

This leads me to the subject of environmental policy. Here, I think, we have a fundamental problem with our approach to pollution control which must be corrected if we are ever to solve energy and environmental problems simultaneously.

The problem is inherent in the approach of setting emissions effluent standards and then enforcing against them. This approach was fine when I was at the Environmental Protection Agency (EPA), because it works well for gross pollution. Six years ago, that is what we had, and it was easy to find and prosecute the polluter who was grossly out of compliance. The violation of standards—any standard—was clear, and any court could see it.

But things have changed. Most industrial polluters, at least, are on the road to compliance, if not there already. And as we get closer to compliance, the standards and enforcement approach works less well. Standards must be more precise since violations are harder to detect, and courts are harder to persuade. As a result, the system has begun to break down, in two ways.

- First, it has become impossibly complex. Standards become more elaborate, and data requirements to prove violations become immense. Equity becomes a problem, leading to such complexities as the nonattainment policy. Frustration with this complexity leads to ideas such as BACT—designed to cut through the maze of regulations by imposing a technological requirement that may not be needed.

- Second, and perhaps more important, the system distorts resource allocation. Standards are imposed externally to the market system, thereby giving up the best resource allocator of all. Worse, disconnecting pollution control from the market system also disconnects it from the energy system. In the long run, I suggest that this broken link will substantially inhibit both energy and environmental solutions.

The alternative is obvious, if not easy to apply. In order to control pollution we need a system of emission or effluent fees. Only such a system truly internalizes environmental costs. Only such a system is likely to optimize resource allocation. It completes the environment–energy–economic linkage. And most important, it is at least as simple as the increasingly unworkable system we now have.

Environmental protection is more than pollution control, of course. It also encompasses the way in which we use our land and water. And here we also have a problem. We plan for land and water use poorly. The fact that we have poor planning systems for land and water use is hardly news. What is news, however, is that we are doing such planning in the absence of good systems and are likely to make some bad mistakes.

A good example is the policy of nondegradation. It is, in plain and simple language, a land use-planning policy. But it is land use planning based on a single objective—the preservation of air quality. It is a noble goal, but hardly the sole one for land use. The longer we pursue it, the more errors we will make.

As long as we do not understand the need to deal comprehensively with our land and water, our environment, and our energy needs, we are destined to continue acting as though every environmental issue were independent of its brothers. We struggle with each problem as though it were the first, and make each policy choice as though it were the last. Then another crisis grabs our attention and we begin again.

Why should it be this way? Why should our energy policies be shortsighted, our pollution control systems be increasingly ineffective, and our land and water use planning be hopelessly inadequate, if not outright counterproductive?

I think that the answer lies in part within the nature of our institutions. For, in the EPA, and now in the Department of Energy (DOE), we have not only created new institutions, but radically different ones. They are problem-solving institutions, created to right a major national ill to the exclusion of all others. And if they stray from their issue too far, their congressional and public constituencies quickly right the course.

Because of their narrow focus and constituency pressure, such agencies behave in odd ways. They discriminate, for one thing. The EPA goes after big polluters and the DOE after big oil companies. They have their hit lists, because they have to show results and stand up to the bad guys.

Such institutions are less than likely to take the long view, for their dedication to their issue is tested daily. Such institutions are not prone to find ways of working through economic incentives; it is too invisible a role. Such institutions probably will not engage in tradeoffs, because someone's ox will get gored. It is instructive to recall the outrage that greeted the notion of a Department of Energy and Environment. But maybe it is what we should have had.

Well, so much for energy imperatives and the environment. There are energy imperatives—resources we must use in order to avoid an energy shortage. Their exploitation may exhaust our environmental resources before our energy sources run dry. And we lack the energy policy, the environmental processes, and the institutions that may be needed to bring energy and environment back into balance.

Perhaps I am too pessimistic. But after nearly six years of close proximity to energy and environmental issues, I cannot be sanguine. Yet, there could be no subject about which an understanding of our resources for the future is more important. Let me commend this institution for attacking the problem twenty-five years ago and wish you success in tackling what promise to be even tougher problems for the future.

Coping with an Uncertain Future—Three Assessments

Historical Perspective
William H. McNeill

Professor of History, University of Chicago

Human history is nothing more nor less than a record of change. It follows that coping with change—the title assigned to the deliberations of this panel—is but another name for the human condition. Problems of food and fuel supply, which loom large in our consciousness today, are not without historical parallels, sometimes remarkably close, as in the case of the seventeenth-century Mediterranean food and fuel crisis that set in with the widespread exhaustion of forests adjacent to that sea. The main difference, it seems to me, is that we in the fourth quarter of the twentieth century are far better informed and can see the disaster coming in a way that earlier generations, similarly threatened, seem not have done. This enhances anxiety in some quarters and induces indifference in others, but it is surely arguable that foresight and anticipation may assist in preparing alternatives and make more likely a successful response to critical shortages. At any rate, the *raison d'être* of this organization, Resources for the Future, consists of that hope.

William H. McNeill

The Consolation of History

If we employ a long enough time scale, humanity's career upon earth looks like the progress of a
band of brachiating apes through the forest, leap-
ing from branch to branch, that is, from one
ecological niche to another. From time to time, an
overloaded branch cracks; bodies sometimes fall
to their death; but always, at least so far, new
branches have somehow come within reach, and
the band swings on.

Our remotest, fully human ancestors began
the adventure by climbing to the top of the food
chain as the most formidable of hunters. Humankind then proceeded to exterminate many of the
large-bodied game animals upon which the hunters were accustomed to prey. This Paleolithic
crisis provoked experiments in food production
in many different parts of the earth, beginning
about 8000 B.C. or so; and in about a dozen local-
ities, sufficiently productive crops and domesticated species of animals were developed to
allow the emergence of new and far more popu-
lous forms of human society. This change has
often been called the Neolithic revolution.

A bit later, the first civilization, based on irri-
gation agriculture, arose in the floodplain of the
Tigris–Euphrates. About a thousand years there-
after, salting of the fields resulting from evapora-
tion brought on a new kind of crisis that required
abandonment of the original city sites and reloca-

tion of civilized social structures upriver—first, at Babylon, then still further north in Assyria. More significant than this relocation was the gradual emancipation of civilized life from the flood-plains and its domestication on rain-watered land. This occurred about the year 2000 B.C. and made civilization of the Near Eastern variety potentially endemic throughout the relatively broad regions of the earth where soils and climate allowed the production of a food surplus by peasant farmers, using their own muscles and those of a few domesticated animals for the tasks of cultivation.

A couple of thousand years later a new kind of ecological disaster hit wide regions of the by-then-civilized world of Eurasia. I refer to the exposure of large populations to new and formidable epidemic diseases. The resulting die-off in both China and the Roman Empire, where surviving records allow reasonably precise estimates, were severe and, together with barbarian invasions and civil disorders, led to widespread decay of civilized forms of social organization. The resulting Dark Age lasted for several centuries in Western Europe; but in time recovery did come, probably quite as rapidly as recovery from the Paleolithic food disaster. Global history, accordingly, witnessed first a rise of the East, as China attained leadership in almost every aspect of civilized life, and then a rise of the West, when

Europe followed suit and swiftly expanded its range of action over all the world.

Yet Europe's rise was by no means one long uninterrupted record of material progress. Local disasters, sometimes involving setbacks lasting for centuries, abound. The decay of German cities during and after the Thirty Years' War is a familiar example; the collapse of Dutch prosperity under the burden of the French wars is another. The decay of Italian cities after the first decades of the seventeenth century is a less familiar instance, since it was not tied in directly with warfare; but details have recently been worked out by a brilliant cluster of French historians. Of course these disasters were local. In each case, in an adjacent part of Europe, conditions were such that a continued growth of technology, or organizational skill, and of knowledge could and did occur. From sufficient remove, therefore, the whole process looks like a single upthrust, recurrently raising human power and wealth to higher and higher levels.

The consolation of history, then, for those harried men who seek to cope intelligently with the looming food and fuel crisis of the twentieth and twenty-first centuries is short and simple: we are not unique; you are not alone. Human beings have often confronted analogous situations and, so far at least, have always found new ecological niches that, in fact, allowed more people to share the surface of planet Earth than had before been possible.

This is not a trifling consolation, it seems to me, and I strongly recommend Fernand Braudel's famous work *The Mediterranean in the Age of Philip II* as bedside reading for anyone worried about the oil problem we face today—for it was he, more than anyone else, who illuminated the dilemmas facing Mediterranean people and states immediately before and after 1600 when supplies of wood began to run low.

Ambivalence of Our Position

All the same, I would like to also emphasize ways in which our situation differs from what earlier generations faced. As I said already, the first difference is that we know so much. As far as I am aware, earlier ecological–economic disasters were not foreseen; or if foreseen by humble technicians of some sort, their views did not reach, or were not taken seriously, by political and cultural leaders, and accordingly left no trace in available records. Untoward developments were, characteristically, attributed to supernatural action. The Will of God explained everything that happened and may sometimes have discouraged mere human effort to head off disaster. Given the realities of life in a time when vagaries of weather ruled the harvest, and when raids and ravaging by who knew what unfamiliar band of ruffians was an ever-present possibility, any explanation of things that did not emphasize the unexpected and uncontrollable aspect of experience would have been utterly at odds with life as actually lived. It is not surprising, therefore, that divine retribution for past transgression was the only explanation human beings found plausible when some new disaster overtook them. Since the seventeenth century, however, a few European visionaries, calling themselves natural philosophers, propounded the notion of a world machine whose movements were, or ought to be, predictable. Such "scientific" views challenged older, providential interpretations of reality, and govern most of thought today, despite the fact that human experience has yet to be reduced to predictable proportions.

Nevertheless, we are always probing the limits of understanding, and disseminate data relentlessly. We extrapolate and exaggerate and cry "Wolf, wolf!" And when that does not get attention, try something still more shrill in the hope of galvanizing the public into action. Whether this noisy concern for the future will sharpen reactions and improve chances of an effective response when real shortages arise remains to be seen. But we will be conscious of the process as our predecessors seldom or never were; of that we can be sure. I suppose the chances of a successful response are increased rather than diminished by this fact, despite the distractions that competing voices create.

A second difference between our situation and that of any preceding generation facing an impending ecological crunch is likewise ambiguous in its augury for future success. I refer to the fact that the wealthier countries of the world today have pretty well destroyed the old, peasant agricultural class upon which earlier civilizations rested. This meant an enormous increase in efficiency and a rise in living standards. It also means that if the web of exchange that nourishes our cities and sustains our farming should ever come to a halt for as much as six months, the resulting disaster would be enormous. Aforetime, when about four-fifths of the population raised its own food and produced locally almost everything it consumed, cities and civilization could rise and fall and affect the lives of the rural majority only marginally. Consequently, the social basis for rebuilding an urban civilization lay ready at hand, no matter what kind of disaster city folk might experience.

Today it is still true that more than half of humankind exists at a peasant level, enjoying (and suffering from) local self-sufficiency for most critical items of consumption. But in the Western world it is not so, and our enhanced vulnerability to any prolonged interruption of exchange patterns is correspondingly great. We have traded wealth and power for assured survival in time of disaster. It remains to be seen how the tradeoff will balance out across, say, a thousand years.

On the other hand, the regenerative capacity of modern industrial–commercial society is extraordinary. The recovery of Germany and Japan from World War II is a telling demonstration of what can be done when conditions are right. Yet their recoveries depended on transfusions from outside. If a truly global disaster should descend upon us, so that all existing high-technology societies suffered as much as several months' interruption of the exchange of goods and services that keep them alive, then regeneration would not be easy and might be impossible for centuries. Thus our enhanced powers are profoundly ambivalent as far as I can see. It has always been so, however. Every new skill brings new risks; and humanity has been accumulating skills and risks at an unprecedented pace lately.

Beyond Statistics

What the upshot may be, time alone will tell. Historians are only good for hindsight—and rather coarse-grained hindsight at that, especially when put into juxtaposition, as in this panel discussion, with the modes of analysis to which economists are accustomed. Yet I believe historians' preoccupation with catastrophe might be useful to economists, if they care to listen. Extreme cases, breakdowns, abrupt interruptions of established market relations—these are not staples of economic theory, and are, I believe, usually dismissed by statistically minded analysts of the norm and its fluctuations. But human societies are a species of equilibrium, and equilibria are liable to catastrophe when, under special limiting conditions, small inputs may produce very large, often unforseen, and frequently irreversible outputs. I believe there is a branch of mathematics that deals with catastrophe—sudden changes in process; I must say that I, as an historian contemplating the richly catastrophic career of humanity across the centuries, venture to recommend to economists a more attentive consideration of such models—at least when trying to contemplate the deeper past and long-range future.

Scientific Perspective
Lewis M. Branscomb

Vice President and Chief Scientist, IBM Corporation

My message is a simple one: technology can give
us plenty of alternatives. But coping with an uncertain future requires a healthy respect for the
unpredictability of nature and the limitations of
our knowledge. Our problem is not fear of technology, but an unwillingness to face up to the
responsibilities that go with its opportunities.

People today are dismayed at forecasts of a
bleak future of exhausted resources and social
turmoil on a polluted, overpopulated planet. Yet,
the technophobes are outnumbered by those who
ask too much from science and technology. We are
told that we have a right to expect a better future
than previous generations ever thought was possible, let alone was their right to demand. However you may choose to measure the quality of life,
or weigh the maldistribution of the most valued
benefits—there has certainly been a revolution of
expectations.

Indeed, from a global point of view, the revolution in expectations for more widely shared access to the fruits of technology is fueled by falling
death rates, increased urbanization, and the ac-
cessibility of global communications. Political
turbulence in the Third World is a reflection of

these expectations. At home the scientific community shudders at the phrase "war on cancer," implying that the expenditure of public money is the only substantial obstacle to the elimination of this disease. We are told that there is enough coal and fissionable material to last us many decades. When these run out, technologies for solar, fusion, and biological fuel systems can be invoked. It is just a matter of time and permissive cost. Why, then, do we seem to be losing the first battle in what President Carter calls the "moral equivalent of war"? The so-called energy crisis and, indeed, most of the other crises that are overloading the consensus-making institutions in our democracy, are crises of confidence and will. These crises result when the positive potential of technological alternatives encounters the limitations of both centralized (public policy) and decentralized (competitive market) mechanisms for decision making.

Obviously, we—collectively—are not managing our affairs well. Maybe we never did, but now the circumstances are different. Today there is something we can do about many of our problems. That something derives from the potential of new technology. Thus, I contend that while future shock from coping with the social consequences of technological change does make it harder for a lot of people to cope, the real problem is coping with the gap between what is and what could be.

The problems are thus primarily political, social, and economic. But if the stress that results from coping in these spheres proves too traumatic, the result may be to suppress the very resources of science and technology that give rise to the new expectations in the first place.

Overburdening the Courts

The case that a democracy may be fatally stressed by conflicting values and expectations born of new possibilities deserves a careful hearing. Our government was designed deliberately to make decisions difficult. Divided authority and protection of minority views are our first defense against tyranny. Conducting the government's business is a complex process of consensus building. It is no wonder that most of our senators, congressmen and executives in government are lawyers. They are trained to master complex facts quickly, if superficially, and to search for the common denominator of action that will resolve conflicts. Where conflicting views cannot be accommodated, the problem is somehow ducked or postponed. Reducing or containing conflict is, after all, the first priority in a democracy. Planning for an uncertain future must come second.

I believe that this explains why such a large burden for resolving scientific and technological issues in public policy has been thrown on the courts. The National Environmental Protection Act (NEPA) is, in my view, the most significant and far-reaching legislative innovation of the past quarter-century. It has made the courts a primary instrument for balancing incommensurate values—weighing the survival of the Furbish Lousewort against economic development in Maine, to assessing the need for fuel in central states against the fear of pollution in our coastal ports and shores. Unhappily, the courts traditionally look backward to precedent and to established fact; they are ill-equipped to look into the future in order to deal with statistical uncertainty and damages or benefits yet to be realized. But even if our judges were equipped to generate the information required to guide today's actions in light of future consequences, I fear for the ultimate consequences to our most cherished political values. The judiciary can serve as a political safety valve only up to a point. Beyond that point the responsibility must come back to the people directly.

Thus, a well-informed electorate is the ultimate safeguard of our liberties, as indeed it has always been. But today, a substantial amount of scientific and technological literacy must be added to the growing burden of citizen responsibilities. What then should the citizen's view of the prospects for mankind be? We had better start with the myth of finite resources.

Lewis M. Branscomb

Finite Resources and Human Potential

To be sure, the material resources of the planet are finite, although in any practical sense the most abundant minerals in the earth's crust are effectively inexhaustible. There are specific materials that are—or could soon be in short supply—oil, chromium, and so forth. But we must remember that the reason they are in potentially short supply is a reflection of the particular mix of technologies that constitute our *de facto* technology strategy for materials. In fact, the spectrum of materials strategies made possible by science is so broad and is expanding so fast that it is very difficult to identify any function served by technology for which alternative materials solutions cannot be found.

The point is that the planet is *physically* finite. Its renewable, living resources are not only finite in amount, but may be irreversibly exhausted if their ecological balance is fatally upset. But the resource of physical and human resources, taken together, is open-ended as far as we know. In the language of the systems analyst, managing resources in the future is not a "zero sum game." Every action does not have to result in an eventual negative consequence of comparable magnitude. Energy can be traded off against not only materials, but even intangibles like information. Information is the ultimate renewable resource. Indeed, it improves and spreads in the very process of consumption. Thus the scope of choice open to mankind is determined not only by the material resources available today, but the hard and soft technologies that exist and can be generated for the future.

Even if convinced that our options are quite open-ended, it does not follow that coping with future uncertainty is made easier as a consequence. Indeed, the more options there are, the more uncertain is the course of future events. Choice is a precondition to coping; it is necessary but not sufficient. Private choice among many alternatives in a competitive enterprise environment will doubtless best satisfy the immediate needs and desires of the public. But the scale of human activity is such that private choice must operate within a context that is compatible with the future survival of human society under acceptable conditions. This context must account for the fact that human activity may transform the natural environment in irreversible ways. Changing fossil fuel to carbon dioxide may have climatological consequences of a seriously threatening character. By the time a statistically significant change in carbon dioxide concentration in the atmosphere is unambiguously established, it may be too late to avoid a deleterious effect on food production, for example. Of course, we do not know for certain that this would be the result of an energy strategy that emphasizes exploitation of coal reserves and effectively foregoes the nuclear option. And there are hazards associated with the nuclear alternative. But such issues must be faced, and decisions must be made before irreversible harms are suffered—even before science can prove to everyone's satisfaction that predictions of such effects can be relied on.

Zero Risk Versus Lost Opportunity

A second kind of long-term threat to our well-being must also be addressed. The highly complex arrangements that constitute the infrastructure of a modern industrial society are designed for efficiency, but not always for resiliency. Some hard lessons have been taught us by experience with electric power distribution. We have paid less attention than we should to the manner in which the man-made, as well as natural, environments respond to unlikely events. Arrangements that degrade slowly and are resilient to catastrophe are not necessarily hard to provide. They require flexibility, which can be obtained by technological options and appropriate institutional arrangements.

If, indeed, the issues we must face about the future involve substantial uncertainties and if we cannot identify where all the benefits and burdens may fall, how can sensible national and global strategies be generated? I have a few specific suggestions, which were contained in the report of the Bellagio Conference of the National Academy of Sciences in 1976.

Environmental impact statements and the notion of technology assessment, as currently practiced, seek to anticipate the consequences of human activity prior to the introduction of a technology about which we have little experience. Obviously, one should try to be as well informed as possible on the basis of projections, models, and theory. But we must find a way to permit the introduction of technological change in a prudent and graduated manner so that useful knowledge is gained early, and the technology can be evolved with the course of future events. Much recent legislation is written as though zero risk were a sensible goal. But the cost of lost opportunity carries its own risk. To learn what options are useful we must commit ourselves to quantify risks and benefits. That process itself cannot be without risk. We need more measurements and less guess work.

The second need is for improved public understanding. It is not sufficient for experts to advise the leadership. Unless the public understands the reasons for postponing early benefits for long-term safety or gain, the public simply will not allow the leadership—however well informed and enlightened—to make the hard decision. Thus public consensus—not political courage—stands between the scientists and engineers and their opportunity to contribute. When one considers the difficulty of arousing the public's attention and concern over matters of potential importance in the future, one can understand why most scientists fail in their attempts to communicate through the media. But the public measures scientific credibility by a standard unfamiliar to many scientists; that is, the ability to dramatize and simplify when communicating outside the group of recognized experts in one's field. This situation offers opportunities, but also temptations which can lead to corruption of the integrity of the scientific process.

The Financial and Institutional Challenge

Finally, early warning is not enough. We must develop institutions under a variety of sponsorships and arrangements to provide the facts and analysis required for anticipatory decisions. Such problem-oriented institutions should undertake substantive scientific, economic, and policy research and must be experienced and credible enough to deal with problems so riddled with uncertainties and hypothetical situations. Modeling the future as the basis for public decisions today is not a part-time or weekend task. There are few such institutions in the United States today; Resources for the Future is one of them. Why has the evident need not been filled?

The answer is that we have not developed a satisfactory way of financing this kind of research. The job to be done may be too big for private philanthropy alone, although some foundations have made an impressive start. Government appropriations are not the proper way to fund independent research that bears so directly on the balancing of values and interest, since government agencies, no less than private interests, have a way of knowing how the answers ought to come out. The Executive Branch agencies are parties at interest. The courts and the Congress need independent sources of analysis and expert testimony. To reduce the stress on the political process and to strengthen the public's ability to make informed choices, private initiative and support are essential.

Economic Perspective
Paul W. MacAvoy

Professor of Economics, Yale University

On the twenty-fifth anniversary of the founding of Resources for the Future, a great deal can be said about concern for the nation's resources that is not alarmist, overstated, or misplaced. The founding of RFF, following the Paley Commission's report, was called for on the premise that in a few decades the wolf would be at the door. On this anniversary, it is appropriate to indicate that the wolf is out there, but that he could well be held at bay for a while longer. The nation's resources, while more depleted and in shortage in some cases, have not been misused in ways that have reduced the capacity of the American economy, even though many of RFF's strictures and proposals for efficient use have been ignored.

Coping with the Gas Crisis

Certainly one of the most severe "shortages" in the nation's history, if not the worst, occurred in Ohio in January and February of 1976. Weather conditions across the nation were worse than in any winter in a hundred years, and natural gas deliveries were curtailed by the Columbia Gas

System to almost all factories, municipal build-ings, and school systems in Ohio. The shortage was dealt with by substitution of other fuels, re-arrangement of work schedules and school oper-ations to times when fuels were not so necessary, and by simply reducing rates of consumption of energy of one kind or the other.

This shortage and its concomitant manage-ment by the company, state regulatory commis-sions, and the Federal Power Commission had been long foreseen by RFF's staff and other en-ergy analysts in universities, corporations, and government agencies. Drastic policy measures had been proposed to prevent the shortage from occurring—such as the elimination of federal controls over prices and production of natural gas at the wellhead in the Southwest. But, rather than carry out such a measure, which the senators from Ohio regarded as a rip-off of Ohio citizens through producer price increases, the politics called for muddling through the winter with stopgap measures to manage the shortage. The results were to reduce employment and pro-duction by substantial amounts throughout the Ohio economy. But most of the losses, even in employment, were made up in the subsequent few months. The residual, in fact, mostly con-sisted of an outbreak of further state and national investigations of the competence of the Columbia

Gas System and of the allegation that producers were "withholding" gas during the freezing months of winter. Ultimately, additional legislation was enacted at the state level, calling for public divulgence of plans, prospects, and sources of supply of the Columbia Gas System. But there was, in fact, no sustained and disruptive shortage, and the immediate events had little effect on Ohio's economy in 1976.

Impact of Price Controls

The simple sequence of policy steps taken in recent years to manage natural gas crises follows the path leading to the very resource misuse or waste that was discussed in the Paley Commission's report. The exploration and development of gas supplies has proceeded from the most productive and advantageously located formations to those less well endowed, with the result that the marginal supply costs have been rising rapidly over time (possibly at the rate of 20 to 25 percent per annum). At the same time, the opportunity costs of the exploratory process have gradually shifted from gains foregone on shallow onshore drilling in such locations as the Panhandle of Texas to gains foregone on North Sea, West African, and Southeast Asian offshore drilling platforms (whose crude oil prices reach fifteen dollars or more per barrel).

Thus, while the costs of additional gas supplies have probably quadrupled in the last ten years, prices have not increased by anywhere near this magnitude, since they have been controlled by the FPC under court mandates since 1954. Price levels before 1970 barely exceeded $1.00 per barrel and annual increases did not keep up with the general rate of inflation. More recently, gas prices have approached levels one-half those of international crude oil, or roughly $8.50 per barrel crude oil equivalent. The price controls have bred profligacy in the use of natural gas on the part of industrial users of boiler fuel who have "grandfather" rights to supplies obtained in the 1950s. They also provided supplies to home consumers for heating at high temperatures, for extensive air conditioning, and for new uses such as ornamental lanterns, outdoor barbecue facilities, and saunas for customers connected to the so-called low-cost retail gas utilities. The only problem was the shortage creation inherent in the expanding demands. The depletion and profligate demands were met after 1970 by lessening supplies, until shortages developed to the extent of 20 percent of total demands.

It has taken almost twenty years for this misuse of scarce national resources to be made evident. The country has been left with a smaller stock of natural gas, while a wide variety of fore-

casters and prognosticators—including RFF—
were pointing out the likelihood that there were
more than sufficient, undiscovered and unde-
veloped reserves to replenish the stock, and perhaps even to hold it level for the rest of the
century.

It is likely that this type of regulatory policy
will be followed for other natural resources in the
next two decades. As new deposits become more
scarce and market prices rise, federal actions to
prevent further price increases will be taken to
avoid wealth or income losses on the part of
those consuming the original stock, whether they
be corporation or final consumer.

All of this will lead to excess demand, waste
in the use of resources, and short-term disruptions in the operations of the national economy.
Some of these effects may be marginally important. The natural gas shortage probably has, for
example, been important not because of last winter's rationing—the effects were transitory, as has
been argued—but because it has accounted for
most of the increase in imports of foreign crude
oil, which in turn accounts for the East Coast's
increasing vulnerability to embargo and disruption for short periods by OPEC nations. The
wastage of resources under price controls breeds
entrenchment and privilege, which has far-
reaching effects, including the wider application
of Nelson's Law (that is, the further away an

economy moves from market equilibrium, the less likely it will ever return because interest groups operating under the disequilibrium have much more to lose from such a return).

Coping with Another Embargo

Consider once again the probable impact of a significant embargo of the U.S. market by crude oil producers in the Middle East within the next few years. This would cause a significant diminution in supply, over a period ranging from one month up to one year, depending on how well the restriction and specification of purchaser would work over that period. This would cause a 10 percent reduction in total energy supplies, which—assuming fixed input–output relations—could in the extreme reduce the GNP by no more than half that percentage. But some part of that GNP would be much more valuable in final consumption than others, and those users with higher-valued output would bid away the remaining and more scarce supplies so that the price would increase and real GNP would decrease by far less than this percentage.

This is the likely sequence of events for a supply disruption in a natural resource over the coming decades. There are many ways in which it profits individuals and corporations to hold stocks against shortages or price increases,

whether the commodities are coffee, energy resources, or bauxite deposits. Where the incentives to reduce risk of depletion are dampened by
government controls—controls that prevent one
from profiting from having held resources or
materials—then there may be insufficient hold-
ings. But these insufficiencies, as in natural gas,
are not now nor can they ever be significant from
the point of view of the economy as a whole. If
they were to seriously threaten a recession, the
governments themselves would either change
the controls or begin holding stocks of resources
(something governments seem attracted toward
doing in any case).

Impact on Growth

Then, what is the concern with resource
policies? The underlying issue is whether the
path of GNP growth is steep or shallow—whether
the rate of growth of the economy is kept some-
where near maximum level or allowed to be
much less. The rate of growth depends upon investment in capital equipment, the rate of technical progress in capital and labor, and the level
and growth of the labor force. That the wolf of
depletion is at the door in natural gas, crude oil,
and materials affects investment and technical
progress. Investment is not for what would be
more productive supplies of materials but rather

is merely to replace aged and depleted stocks. More has been invested in projects to work around bottlenecks produced by the policy process in liquified natural gas, foreign natural gas pipelines, and non-OPEC foreign well drilling. This policy has induced the marginal productivity of energy investments and because of the importance of energy in the economy has thusly reduced the productivity of all investments.

To some extent, the new investment pattern has reduced the trend rate of growth of the American economy. What was a 4 percent growth path through most of the period since World War II has probably been reduced to a shallower path, somewhat closer to 3 percent per annum in the level of the real GNP. Some part of the reduction is due to reduced capital outlays, consequent upon the uncertainty and lower profitability of capacity in energy supplies and in raw materials generally. The contemporary consumers receive lower-priced (but higher-cost) supplies of resources at the expense of further generations who will find levels of the GNP lower after the turn of the century than they would have been if resources had been used more efficiently in more open markets in the 1970s. The wolf can explain this complicated matter to our grandchildren.

Environment and the Economy: Managing the Relationship

Charles L. Schultze
Chairman, Council of Economic Advisers

The theme I want to emphasize can be briefly stated: the achievement and the preservation of a reasonably clean and healthy environment imposes a set of requirements on the social institutions and the political skills of a free society that are both extremely demanding and significantly different from those that have served us well for other purposes in the past. I do not believe that we have yet developed the necessary institutions, or the necessary social skills; and as a consequence we are having now, and will continue to have, substantial difficulties in meeting our environmental goals while still preserving other economic and political values that we esteem very highly. Nor do I think that the solutions will become any easier as we move through the next twenty-five years toward RFF's Golden Jubilee.

When I talk about the environment, what I mean is not the environment in the narrow sense —not just clean air and water—but environmental esthetics, health and safety in the workplace, and the characteristics of the products we consume. More generally, I am talking about what we economists call the problem of externalities—that is, how to control the unwanted side effects of our production and consumption decisions. But I will concentrate on the problems of the environment as it is more narrowly described.

At the risk of some oversimplification, the role of the government in the United States—particularly the federal government—until recently was confined principally to a limited sphere of activities. These include producing or supporting the production of goods that private enterprise could not or should not handle; enforcing the rules of the game through contract law and antitrust policies; redressing through taxes and transfer payments the maldistribution of income; and for one reason or another, regulating a highly select sphere of private activities, such as transportation, electric utilities, and financial institutions.

But the chief characteristic of environmental and other health and safety side effects is that they are not restricted to any well-defined set of activities. Indeed, they are pervasive, running throughout the private production and consumption decisions of millions of business firms and hundreds of millions of consumers.

Ours is a highly affluent, urbanized, technologically advancing, economically dynamic, and chemically inventive society. And every one of these characteristics contributes to the magnitude and pervasiveness of environmental side effects. As we have grown more affluent, we have demanded more. When we earn our daily bread by the sweat of our brow, amenities are not very important. But environmental amenities become terribly important, the less we sweat and the more bread we have.

Urban conglomerations themselves tend to concentrate environmental damages and increase the likelihood of other side effects. Sheer physical closeness is an important cause of environmental problems. And because we are technologically advancing, we create not only new production techniques, but also new ways of despoiling the environment. And because we are a dynamic economy, firms and production processes are constantly shifting about, so that environmental standards in any one location—and in every location—have to change to accommodate the birth and death of firms and establishments. And finally, because we are chemically inventive, we are continually increasing the numbers of new chemical compounds whose yet unknown side effects may be dangerous.

The problem is not merely, or even principally, technological, nor is it even principally *economic* in the fundamental sense of the term. Devising technical solutions is not our problem. Our problems are really social and political. If there are limits to growth, the limits to growth are not going to arise from technological or re-source factors. The limits to growth—and, in some very fundamental sense, the limits to choice as we try to handle these problems—are going to be determined by our ability to devise social institutions and to develop social skills capable of dealing with these kinds of pervasive problems.

How does society deal with such side effects, which are numerous, complex, pervasive, and acting on all our lives in different ways every day? How can we shape millions of individual deci-sions effectively toward social ends without strangling our other goals, especially economic growth and reasonable freedom of choice? How do we deal with millions of location decisions, changes in technologies and processes, and raw materials choices? What goods should be pro-duced? What chemicals, fertilizers, and dyes should we allow or not allow, discourage or not discourage?

I do not pretend to have the answers to these questions, but I do want to suggest three direc-tions in which we might move.

Commands or Incentives?

The first of these has to do with the way in which we as a society intervene in order to deal with environmental and other side effects. We usually tend to see but one way to solve such problems: we remove them from the decentralized, incentive-oriented market system and transfer them to a hierarchical command-and-control bureaucracy.

This seems such a clear-cut and simple way to do things. If you want to get something done —if you want, say, to reduce a polluting effluent —then specify the limits on that effluent for every firm that might put it into a river or into the air. Sometimes, specify the techniques of production. Sometimes, specify the raw materials to be used. Sometimes, specify what kind of treatment is to be given at the end of the pipe, or the chimney. In general, go at it in what appears to be a straightforward way; that is, determine what outcome is wanted, and by laws and regulations command that such an outcome be achieved.

And yet, this direct, hierarchical, command-and-control approach often is incapable of dealing with the complex problems we are trying to solve—precisely because we are dealing with such pervasive phenomena—millions of decisions under widely differing circumstances of costs and technology and raw materials, in widely differing regions, and reflecting widely differing tastes.

In a long series of studies, RFF has contrasted this command-and-control approach with an alternative form of social organization, one that attempts to use incentives and self-interest to achieve the common good. Essentially, what this second approach involves is recognizing that environmental damages are costs, and that in the normal course of economic life those who use scarce resources are required to pay the cost of those resources. It relies upon self-interest to achieve the kind of results we want. Elsewhere this approach has been elaborated at great length, and I am not going to repeat it here, but I do want to stress several points.

First, the incentive-based approach has limits. It is not a panacea. Although, on the whole, it does work, it cannot handle many kinds of problems. Where we are dealing not with questions of more or less, but of absolute zero, then the incentive system is unnecessarily complex. In such circumstances it is simpler to use regulations to ban or forbid. Some of the stickiest problems that must be faced in the future will be in the use of new chemicals and possible carcinogens. And here the fundamental problem, before we get to social institutions, is that we really do not understand their effects; we are faced with great uncertainty. And I, at least, do not know of any social system—large or small—that deals very well with problems of extremely large and highly uncertain damages. The kinds of decentralized, incentive-oriented institutions that might work well in many ways also are very difficult to apply here. But since that is also true of any system, I must—as the old Scots preacher said, coming to a difficult passage in the Bible—"look this difficulty firrrmly in the face and pass on."

Second, we are not starting from scratch in trying to introduce decentralized, incentive-oriented systems into handling the environment. We are starting with a complex of existing laws and regulations, and of interests, accomplishments, and failures, which are based pretty much on the hierarchical command-and-control technique. Even if we could reach an agreement, we cannot junk the existing system and substitute an alternative approach. Instead we have to find ways to make a gradual transition over the years from what we have now to what it is absolutely essential that we have in the years to come.

Finally, an incentive-oriented approach is really an attempt to create a new market for a set of valuable commodities that have not been treated in a market sense before: namely, the environment. And yet, we have not had, if you think of it, very much, if any, experience as a society in creating large new markets *de novo*. Most markets that we know about have emerged over time through years and decades—and, in some cases, generations—of trial and error; and the equilibrium that we now observe has resulted over time. How do we go about creating a large new market which—in terms that I described before—is very pervasive and complex?

With all these difficulties, I think we must rely on a different kind of social organization from the one we are now using to deal with the environment. We must do so for one critical reason: the future of our society is going to hinge, in part, on the discovery and adoption of ever-improving technologies in order to reduce the environmental consequences of expanding production. There is no way that we can achieve our purposes, nor in fact, continue to exist as an advancing society, without a continuing shift in the direction of technological change. And this is not a matter of a crash program—a Manhattan Project or a space project. We are dealing with a constant channeling and fostering of certain kinds of technologies relative to others. And it is here that the power of marketlike incentives and the forces of self-interest to stimulate and direct innovation is most critical. To put it another way, the static efficiency of marketlike approaches is small potatoes when compared with the long-term, dynamic efficiency.

Our living standards today are, by orders of magnitude, higher than those of the early seventeenth century. Had the triumph of the market meant merely that we used then-existing technologies more effectively, our increases in living standards would have been minuscule compared with what actually happened. And by analogy, if we look not just at the Golden Jubilee of RFF but at its centenary, then it is precisely that channeling of technology that is so critical. I am convinced that whatever regulation can do, it is extremely inept at pacing and channeling technology. It thus becomes necessary to harness the motivation and self-interest of individuals and firms to carry out this absolutely crucial task.

Setting Environmental Priorities

Let me turn to a second major area, of somewhat less importance, in which I think we can improve the capacity of our social institutions to deal with harmful environmental and other side effects. Over the years, we have developed an information planning and control mechanism through which the federal government, and other levels of government, can deal with the myriad activities that government carries on. We call that mechanism the budget.

Before the Budget and Accounting Act of 1921, individual departments and agencies of the federal government dealt with budget requests on their own, with no central direction. I am given to understand that there was a single clerk at the Treasury who would receive these departmental requests, bundle them up, and deliver them physically to the Congress. The Budget and Accounting Act brought that all together into a single—presumably, at least—presidentially controlled budget plan. This made it possible to look at the aggregate, and the relationships of the parts to the whole. This device has helped us to set priorities and to evaluate the economic impacts both of the aggregate and the pieces.

Nevertheless, it is imperfect. It is principally composed of costs, and, in most cases, we found no good way to measure benefits. But even with those drawbacks, it has become an obviously indispensable tool for setting priorities. Major improvements have been made in it over the years: The accounting techniques and systems have been improved; more informative and better categories have been devised; and all kinds of special analyses have been perfected so that we can look at the impacts of our programs in different cuts—for example, we can look at all the R&D programs together, all construction programs, or all grant-in-aid programs, and so forth.

In recent years, improvements in the congressional budget process have made it possible for the Congress to look at the budget as a whole, rather than piecemeal. And finally, we are beginning—imperfectly, fumblingly, with some hesitation—to introduce five-year budgets and longer-term planning into the budget exercise.

Now let us turn to regulatory activities—that is, regulations to control externalities and environmental activities. We find no analog to the setting of budgetary priorities. Most of the environmental costs are not budgetary costs or governmental costs. Instead they usually are incurred in the first instance by industry and then passed on in the price of the product. Nevertheless, they are real national costs; the resources used for this purpose cannot be utilized for other purposes. Both the benefits and the costs involved are very large. Depending upon how wide one casts one's net, and what particular estimates one uses, they already run into the scores of billions of dollars each year, and they are growing rapidly.

Thus it may be time to think about constructing a framework within which to plan and set priorities for environmental and related programs, analogous to the federal budget for direct-spending programs. The difficulties in doing this are, and would continue to be, formidable. Unlike most budgetary costs, the costs are incurred outside the federal government. It is sometimes very hard conceptually, let alone empirically, to measure cost. What do you do, for example, when an environmental regulation simply causes a shift from the use of one raw material to another? How do you measure the incremental cost? And if you can measure it in one year, what do you do over time once the switch has been made? There are widely varying estimates of the historical costs of our environmental programs, and even wider estimates of future costs. We know that costs in the regular federal budget are hard to project—you have heard of cost overruns—but they would be much harder to estimate here.

In addition to everything else, the normal federal budget is an instrument of explicit accounting control over costs, imposed explicitly on those who actually disburse the monies. And here again, the analogy with environmental costs falls down. Yet, the concept might be both feasible and useful as an informational device, as a planning tool, as an integrating device, and as a way to develop methods of setting priorities for what we want to accomplish and how rapidly it can be done. To a large extent our decisions now are taken piecemeal, not because of feuding agencies or an unwillingness to cooperate, but in many cases because we lack some action-forcing, integrating mechanism. And, imperfect as it is, the budget does force some such integration and cooperation.

Initially, the data for setting environmental priorities would be very rough and, if not used with great care, could be very misleading. The appropriate categories would have to be developed and would undoubtedly be gross at first.

Nevertheless, the attempt to construct such an instrument might itself produce better estimates and better data.

It is probably true that innovations like this are best developed initially outside government, or certainly outside as well as inside. Environmental control is and must remain a major national priority. Quite probably it does now and will continue to absorb increasing national resources of capital, labor, and materials. And over the years, it will also become increasingly necessary to develop an integrated informational and planning mechanism to guide policymakers in this area. The historical analogy of the budget is one device toward which we might look for such an integrating mechanism. At least, it might make an item for a research agenda both within and outside the government.

Price and Wage Escalation

Let me turn now to the third point I wanted to make, one that is also of a somewhat lower order of priority. It involves the way in which the costs of environmental improvement enter into the wage- and price-setting mechanism. Although a shorter-run problem, it nevertheless is a significant one.

Improving the environment in the broader sense of the term is costly, drawing on resources that could have been used elsewhere. The costs must be paid. But the gains, in the form of environmental improvements, are not captured in our national income and other accounting data generally. Better access to cleaner air, for example, does not show up as an increase in the GNP. What we do when we make environmental improvements is to accept lower economic growth, as conventionally measured, in return for an increment in unmeasured output, or welfare. And if we choose wisely, the national welfare is improved, even if the measured growth in national income is reduced.

Necessarily, we have imperfect measures of national well-being, but since we are aware of this limitation, let us set aside the question of how we determine whether we are better off and turn to a related question, How this process of accepting lower measured growth for increases in welfare intrudes on the setting of wages and prices?

Environmental improvements lead to higher costs of production in the steel industry, the paper industry, or the aluminum industry. They may also increase transportation costs in these industries by shifting plants to less efficient locations. As a consequence, prices of these products rise. We pay a higher price for steel because, in addition to the steel, we are getting some increment in the environmental condition. Higher prices for these products, and for goods that are made from them, will slow down the growth in real wages as they are conventionally measured. That is, precisely because our price indexes reflect environmental costs as well as other costs, the process of improving the environment necessarily means—everything else being equal—that when changes in wages are divided by changes in the consumer price index, the measure of real growth will be lower than it otherwise would be. And this is simply a reflection of the fact that we are giving up some real income—as conventionally measured—for something else.

Over the years we have tried to insulate ourselves from changes in the cost of living. Formal escalators in many wage contracts provide that wages will be raised automatically to compensate for price increases. Other contracts and government programs also escalate various costs, benefits, or remuneration by changes in the measured price indexes. We have developed a partial mechanism for trying to escape the reductions in measured real income growth resulting from price increases, such as those that environmental improvements impose.

As a result of these escalations, environmental improvements impose an additional source of inflationary pressure, not simply in the first round of the price increase, but in subsequent rounds, when the rise in the price index automatically leads to increases in wages and other prices. This increase is not huge. It is not going to bring society to a screeching halt, but it does add to the already difficult set of economic problems that we face. It increases the rigidities in our wage–price mechanism, and makes it more difficult to bring inflation under control during a period in which we are trying to make significant environmental improvements.

I am not suggesting that we change the consumer price index; it measures what it is supposed to measure. It measures the price of steel. If raw material costs go up in steel, we include that rise as an increase in the price; and if environmental improvements—which are a cost—go up, we ought to let it show up in the price of steel. But it might be useful to develop—at least as an educational device—measures of changes in prices and real incomes that exclude the effects of environmental costs.

Again, we face major difficulties. We would have to approximate data, and analytical concepts; but I suggest it might be very useful to develop such indexes in order to indicate what kind of real cost increases are inescapable. Perhaps with a better understanding of the cost of achieving our environmental objectives, we can explore ways to reduce their second- and third-round inflationary impacts.

Appendix

Program for the Forum marking the 25th anniversary of the founding of Resources for the Future, held on October 13, 1977, in Washington, D.C.

Forum Program

Morning Session

Alexander Heard, Chairman of the Board,
Ford Foundation
Chancellor, Vanderbilt University, presiding

Introduction to the Conference
Charles J. Hitch, President,
Resources for the Future

Resources in the Past and for the Future
Edward S. Mason, Dean Emeritus,
Harvard University
Honorary Member, Board of Directors,
Resources for the Future

Emerging Global Resource and Environmental Problems
Harrison Brown, Director
Resource Systems Institute, East-West Center
Member, Board of Directors,
Resources for the Future

Luncheon

Alice M. Rivlin, Director,
Congressional Budget Office, presiding

Energy Imperatives and the Environment
Robert W. Fri, former Deputy Administrator of
the Environmental Protection Agency and the
Energy Research and Development
Administration

104

Afternoon Session

Joseph L. Fisher, Member of Congress
and former President of Resources for the Future,
presiding

Coping with an Uncertain Future Historical, Scientific, and Economic Perspectives
William H. McNeill, Professor of History,
University of Chicago
Lewis M. Branscomb, Vice President and Chief
Scientist, IBM Corporation
Paul W. MacAvoy, Professor of Economics,
Yale University and former Member, Council of
Economic Advisers

Evening Program

Charles J. Hitch, presiding

Reflections on This Day
Gilbert F. White, Professor of Geography,
University of Colorado, Chairman of the Board,
Resources for the Future

Introduction of Speaker
William S. Paley, Chairman of the Board,
CBS, Inc., and former Chairman of the Board,
Resources for the Future

The Environment and the Economy: Managing the Relationship
Charles L. Schultze, Chairman,
Council of Economic Advisers

Resources for an Uncertain Future

$2.95

The papers in this volume were presented in October 1977 at a forum marking the 25th anniversary of the founding of Resources for the Future as a nonprofit research and educational organization. The purpose of the forum was to appraise, from a number of perspectives, the resource and environmental outlook for the United States during the next twenty-five years in the light of events in the recent past.

Charles J. Hitch, the editor, is president of Resources for the Future. The contributors are Lewis M. Branscomb, vice president and chief scientist, IBM Corporation; Harrison Brown, director, Resource Systems Institute, East–West Center; Robert W. Fri, former deputy administrator of the Environmental Protection Agency and the Energy Research and Development Administration; Paul W. MacAvoy, professor of economics, Yale University and former member, Council of Economic Advisers; William H. McNeill, professor of history, University of Chicago; Edward S. Mason, dean emeritus, Harvard University; and Charles L. Schultze, chairman, Council of Economic Advisers.

Published for Resources for the Future

The Johns Hopkins University Press
Baltimore and London

ISBN 0-8018-2098-7